LEFT OF CENTER

Carol Wilging

Dedicated to God

In Loving Memory of Dallas Gene Jones

LEFT OF CENTER

TRUSTING GOD'S PATH DOWN THE ROAD OF LIFE

CAROL WILGING

Left of Center by Carol Wilging
Copyright © 2024 by Carol Wilging
All Rights Reserved.
ISBN: 978-1-59755-808-2

Published by: ADVANTAGE BOOKS™ – Orlando, Florida USA
www.advbookstore.com

All Rights Reserved. This book and parts thereof may not be reproduced in any form, stored in a retrieval system or transmitted in any form by any means (electronic, mechanical, photocopy, recording or otherwise) without prior written permission of the author, except as provided by United States of America copyright law.

Unless otherwise indicated, Bible quotations are taken from the New International Version of the Bible. Copyright© 1973, 1978, 1984 by New York International Bible Society

Library of Congress Catalog Number: 2024943578

Name: Wilging, Carol

Title: Left of Center
Carol Wilging, Author
Advantage Books, 2024

Identifiers: ISBN Paperback: 9781597558082
ISBN eBook: 9781597558198

Subjects: RELIGION: Christian Life – Inspirational

Cover Design by Penelope Mannis

First Printing: August 2024
24 25 26 27 28 29   10 9 8 7 6 5 4 3 2 1

The path of faith is one of sorrow and joy, suffering and healing comfort, tears and smiles, trials and victories, conflicts and triumphs, and also hardships, dangers, beatings, persecutions, misunderstanding, trouble, and distress. Yet "in all these things we are more than conquerors through Him who loved us" (Romans 8:37). Yes, "in all these" – even during storms, when the winds are the most intense – "we are more than conquerors." You may be tempted to run from the ordeal of a fierce storm of testing, but head straight for it! God is there to meet you in the center of each trial. And He will whisper to you His secrets, which will bring you out with a radiant face and such an invincible faith that all the demons of hell will never be able to shake it.

E. A. Kilbourne
Streams in the Desert, July 12

Carol Wilging

Left of Center

1

This is a story of a girl, an average looking, average achieving, average intelligent girl. Raised in middle-class America by Larry & Josephine Tolbert in Akron, Ohio. I had the blessing of having three older sisters, Linda, Patty, and Vicki. Childhood was good, average. Parents that never got divorced. A home filled with love, but far from perfect. A father who did the best he could, even though his best was sometimes harshness with me and my siblings.

We didn't grow up with God in our household. We never went to church as a family, though somehow I attended some Vacation Bible Schools – I thank God for those. But it wasn't until I was about 20 years old and living in Mississippi with my boyfriend, that God began to draw me to Himself. Attending a funeral in Ohio and listening to my coworker, TJ, talk about God and Jesus and His plan for our lives, stirred something in me that led me to know that God was real and that Jesus Christ had died for MY sins and could give me ETERNAL LIFE. So in 1982 I gave my heart and life to the Lord.

Also in 1982, I had a nervous breakdown that led me to a psychiatric ward of a hospital in Pascagoula, Mississippi. That hospitalization brought my parents down to Mississippi, where I saw a side of my dad that neither I, nor any of my siblings, had ever seen. A caring, loving, nurturing side, where he became my strength, a phrase he would use over and over. I'm giving you my strength. After getting out of the hospital and trying to go back to my old life, which didn't exist, because my boyfriend had already found another girlfriend, my mom said one day on the phone, "don't you just want to come home?" I immediately cried, "YES!" So once again my parents drove to Mississippi, and with U-Haul in tow, helped me move back to Ohio.

2

Staying in my parents' home for a few months after moving back to Ohio until I could rest and heal and gain the strength to get on with my life was a huge blessing. In time, I found a good job, found a church, moved into an apartment, and met a man that I thought was "the one for me." We dated for quite a few years until I felt my biological clock ticking and I informed him it was time to get married. He complied. We were married in 1990. My dad had died of a heart attack at the age of 56 in 1987 about three years before we were married, but my mom attended our wedding. I loved Greg deeply, but he didn't share my faith in God, which caused us to have opposing ideas and values about life, so it wasn't long before things began to crumble. After about a year, he cheated on me, and we ultimately divorced in 1992. He had three children, who I adored. I hated that they would have to see their dad go through a second divorce, but it was inevitable and necessary.

Divorcing Greg led me to Doylestown, Ohio, closer to my job. I had found a Nazarene church in Doylestown that helped me grow spiritually and provided me with a strong foundation. I learned the importance of God's Word. At this church I had the opportunity to use my gifts and talents....singing in the choir, singing solos, teaching kids, and helping with administrative things. I began listening to Joyce Meyer on the radio, and I hungered for truth and began reading my bible daily. My mom passed away at the age of 61 in 1992. I had lost both of my parents before I was even 32 years old. Losing my parents changed the family dynamic greatly. Traditions and stability that we had all enjoyed while my parents were alive gradually began to shift. While we still tried to get together at least on holidays, family gatherings became less and less. Our Christmas Eve tradition would never again be the same.

3

In 1994 God led me to a new job as a secretary in Wadsworth, Ohio, which I loved and stayed at for 18 years. In 1993 I joined a bible study with some friends from church that helped me connect and grow with other Christians. After being in this bible study for two years, I had been dating someone, but after we broke up, a friend of mine invited me to go to a small group in Wadsworth that he had been attending, a group for single, divorced, and widowed Christians. It was there that I met Dallas Jones, who was soon to become my husband! A couple months prior to meeting him at this group, where he was a co-leader, I had been at an evening service at a church with some ladies, and they had asked if there was anyone who wanted to come to the altar and be prayed for, specifically with the desire to be married. I went forward, and while being prayed for, I felt a hand on my shoulder. When I looked up to see who it was, there was no-one there. In my spirit, I had a very strong, very real sense, a knowing in my gut, that God had heard my prayer and my heart's desire, and would indeed grant this request, but in His timing; I just had to trust and be patient. My faith that God was going to answer my prayer was very strong. In less than a couple months, I met Dallas.

Our first date was in late April, 1995, and July 4 of the same year he proposed. We were married September 30, 1995. I wouldn't normally recommend marrying so quickly, but it was very clear to both of us that this union was of the Lord. We had both been praying separately for God's will, and we also prayed together, that if this wasn't God's will, that He would let us know. Dallas had two children, Joshua, age 15 and

Jessica, age 12. When we felt we had their blessing, we proceeded with our plans to be married. Dallas had come from a big family, with seven siblings! What a blessing for me to be able to enter into this warm, loving, Christian family, where they welcomed me with open arms. Dallas' parents, Wendell and Wilma Jones, were very kind and loving, and they were very happy for their son and his new wife!

4

I can look back on the photographs from our wedding day in September, 1995, and while there was much joy on our faces and those of our guests, family and friends, there was a different look on the faces of Josh and Jessica, Dallas's children. Sadness would be an understatement. Unless you've experienced the overwhelming ramifications of divorce, you wouldn't understand the pain a child goes through when it becomes clear that mom and dad are not getting back together. I think I represented the proverbial "nail in the coffin" of their parent's marriage, even though they had been divorced for a very long time.

The next several years were a mixture of extreme happiness, coupled with extreme trials and heartache. Dallas and I were madly in love, and God was blessing our relationship. He was the love of my life, and I trusted him completely. We had both learned so much in our previous marriages and ultimate divorces, and we brought our completely whole and healthy selves into this marriage, and it was a beautiful relationship. But as any stepmother can attest, my relationship with his children was filled with some turmoil and heartache. Their unyielding loyalty to their mother would not allow there to be any kind of love toward me. I would beg the Lord to bless my relationship with them. I had never had any of my own children, and I longed to be a part of their lives, and to let them know how much I loved them and their father. Thankfully I had an understanding husband who knew what I was going through and supported me fully. Dallas was also going through some heartache with his kids, because along with their undying loyalty to their mother, came a disconnect with their dad. They had gone through a lot of traumas, and the pain of their parents' divorce and the animosity between their parents left them reeling with thoughts and emotions that they didn't know how to process.

5

Time and God can and did heal the wounds. There were many, many good times and good memories in our new little family; family dinners, playing ball tag and Monopoly, trips to Myrtle Beach and Long Beach, California, birthdays, Christmases, get togethers with Dallas's brother Duane and his family, where Josh & Jessi could hang out with their cousins, and other times together that strengthened our relationships. Over time they saw my love for them and their dad, and my consistent, stabilizing influence helped there to be calm in the midst of the storms of life. Josh came to live with us for a short time in his late teens. We loved having him with us. It helped grow Dallas's relationship with his son. When Jessica was 15 years old, her mom told her she would have to leave and she was 'forced' to come live with us. On the day of her unplanned arrival, she was understandably upset and full of pain and anguish. I took her into my arms to hug her and she let me....and sobbed and sobbed. I immediately thought that perhaps this would ultimately bring a closeness to my relationship with her. Perhaps now God would bless our relationship. Over the next few years, Dallas and I poured all our love and care into her. We wanted her to see a different way to live and to be happy, a life with God in first place of her life. We wanted her to feel safe and secure. She and her brother saw us going to church regularly, and she observed me faithfully reading my bible every morning.

Carol Wilging

6

An unplanned pregnancy by Jessica at the age of 19 brought a baby into our household….Cameron Matthew. First hearing the news that she was pregnant brought shock, anger, fear, and disappointment. We didn't know at the time the very great truth of Genesis 50:20, that what the enemy means for harm, God turns around for good. Cameron was born in March of 2003.

A special relationship began to form as Dallas and I became Grandpa and Grandma to this little guy. After Cameron was born, he and Jessica continued to live with us for two years, and Dallas and I loved having them with us, and we loved watching Jessi grow and blossom into a healthy young woman and mother, and we adored our grandson and the times we got to spend with him. When Cameron was two, Jessica moved out, but didn't go very far – they moved into a duplex rental right across the street, caddy-corner to our home! I was encouraged by that; it seemed she was ready to be out on her own, but by the same token, didn't want to be too far from the love and security she had found with dad and Carol.

What a blessing it was for me, to be able to be Grandma when I had never had the joy of being a mom. When Cameron was outside and would see me, he would jump up & down and yell "Grandma! Grandma! Grandma!" Talk about having your heart melted over and over and over!! Sometimes when I was inside my house I would hear him yell "GRANDMA" and I would immediately be filled with joy and want to run to him. I wanted to be a "safe place" of love and security for him.

In 2005 Jessica once again found herself pregnant and gave birth to another son in April 2006, Anthony Isaac (Tony). Jessi had two children by the time she was 22.

When Cameron was four and Tony was one, life was humming along smoothly. Dallas and I were still extremely happy, we traveled a lot together, Jessica seemed to be doing better, Josh was doing well, we were happy at our church, and spending time with friends and family. But my nice smooth life was about to be turned upside down, in a way I had never expected. In April of 2008 Dallas had a heart attack, and was taken to Akron General Hospital, where they did emergency surgery to insert two stents. Thank God he was going to be alright, and he eventually underwent a cardiac rehab program and we both began to alter our diet. He was doing just great.

7

Dallas bought a motorcycle in 2006, and in July of 2008 we decided to go on a long motorcycle road trip with three other couples who were dear friends. We charted a course of back roads toward Hocking Hills, Ohio where we would rent a cabin and do some hiking. I had no desire to be on the motorcycle for that long, so my friend Ellie and I made the decision to drive my car instead which would enable us to put all the luggage and supplies in the car. Our friends Joe and Cheryl were driving in the lead, followed by Bob and Sue, followed by Jerry, Ellie's husband, and then Dallas. About an hour before our arrival at the cabin, we stopped at a Dairy Queen for ice cream and so the bikers could have some rest. When we got ready to head back on the road, I told Dallas to be the fourth bike, so that I could look at him. After almost 13 years of marriage, he was still my whole world and we were still very much in love.

About 45 minutes went by, when all of a sudden, Dallas started swerving very badly with the motorcycle, and going left of center. I said to Ellie, "what in the world is he doing?!!" Not long after that a beer truck was heading in the opposite direction, and could not stop in time and while Dallas was left of center, the truck collided with him with extreme force. I pulled the car over as quickly as I could, and Ellie and I raced over to where the truck had stopped. I frantically searched for Dallas but could not find him. Finally the driver of the beer truck said, "Ma'am, he's under my truck."

I climbed under the truck and found Dallas laying there unconscious. I just kept repeating "JESUS! JESUS! JESUS!".

He moaned slightly, so I knew that at that moment he was still alive. The next thing I knew there was another person under the truck with me, a man, who said he was a pastor!! I asked him to please pray for my husband!! He appeared out of nowhere, prayed for him, and then he was gone. Was this really an angel?

I heard the sirens approaching, and the next couple hours are somewhat of a blur. Paramedics working on him, my friends and I pacing and praying and crying, trying to make sense of what had just happened. It was truly unbelievable; I felt as if I was in a dream. So surreal. Surely this did not just happen. I couldn't tell you how much time passed, but eventually someone told me that he didn't make it; they had me go see him at the back of the ambulance, so that I could say goodbye. How do you say goodbye to the love of your life, the one that you had prayed for, the answer to years of prayers, the one you trusted and loved more than anyone in the entire world? You can't. You can't say goodbye, not really. Not ever. I carry him in my heart every single day. I had no idea at that moment how my life would forever change.

Because we were three hours from home, we called the owner of the cabin to let them know we wouldn't be arriving, and we found a hotel and spent the night and made the trip back home the next morning. As all of us wives headed back home in my car with my girlfriend driving, I received a phone call from my pastor's wife, Jo-Lynn. She gave me the scripture verse Psalm 139:16 that says "All the days ordained for me were written in your book before one of them came to be." Which comforts me as she explains that "this was his time to go" and God is not unaware. He will be my strength and carry me through this.

8

One of the most difficult things to do after Dallas died was to return home and have to tell our oldest grandson, Cameron, who was five, that his grandpa had died. Tony was only two, and I knew he would never really remember his grandpa. But Cameron and Dallas were super close, and it broke my heart to have to tell him. I asked Jessica to be with me, so we took him into the living room and tried to explain what had happened. He acted very brave. But in a few hours, I could tell the news had finally hit him, and I saw the sadness and despondency on his face. Maybe it was at that moment that my grandma's heart decided it was my job to erase that sadness and try to make him happy.

Over the next few years, we fight to go on with our 'new normal.' I allow myself to mourn and grieve deeply for several years. I would sit on my bed reading my bible and cry and cry, letting the tears flow freely. God met me in those moments, and years of grief and sorrow allowed me to get to know the Comforter, as the Holy Spirit is described in the Bible. How do you get to know the God of All Comfort, without ever having a need to be comforted? There is a song by Casting Crowns called "Voice of Truth" and it says *"but the Voice of Truth tells me a different story, the Voice of Truth says 'do not be afraid.' And the Voice of Truth says 'this is for My glory'. Out of all the voices calling out to me, I will choose to listen and believe the Voice of Truth"*. I would play that song over and over (back when CD's were the way we'd listen to music) and let the tears and the anguish pour out of me. I would come to know that trials and pain and death and heartache are all a part of life, but that God is not unaware. Psalm 34:18 says "The Lord is close to the brokenhearted and saves those who are crushed in spirit." He cares about everything, great or small, that concerns us. I saw a counselor for a short while, having the wisdom to know that witnessing the love of your life get violently hit by a truck while on his motorcycle might just possibly require professional help.

My very favorite bible verse is Romans 8:28 which says that "ALL things work together for good to those who love God and are called according to His purpose." It's always been a comfort that God in His infinite wisdom weaves together all the events and circumstances of our lives into one beautiful tapestry, and is able to bring good out of all things, bringing glory to Himself. While working as a secretary in the office of Freshwater Community Church, I also helped plan the Sunday morning services. I felt led to ask our Pastor if I could share on a Sunday morning how God had been helping me get through Dallas's tragic death. He agreed it would be a great testimony and that he would simply ask me some questions and I would share. The Sunday morning that I spoke of God's faithfulness was August 28, 2011 - 8/28 (Romans 8:28!) It seemed significant to me that THAT would be the day I gave a testimony of how God had brought about comfort and strength through such a horrific tragedy and grief.

Through the early days and months and years of Dallas's passing, my relationship with 5-year old Cameron grew. I think he was helping me grieve, as I was helping him grieve. He just lived across the street, so almost every day he would show up at my doorstep, bringing "new life" back into my soul. We talked about Dallas constantly, my wanting to keep his memory alive and fresh in Cameron's mind. We began making new memories…..too many to count. Our lives intersected. I babysat Cameron and Tony many many times.

One of the very first things I began praying after Dallas died was "Lord, help me be Grandma without Grandpa." How was I to handle this grandparenting role without him? How were they going to have a Godly male influence in their lives? I lost my life partner, the one who would've knelt with me in prayer for them. The one who I could've talked to and shared my heart's concerns for them. The one who was that "extra set of hands" when we babysat them. The one who would put things together that required installation (the one thing I hate doing is reading directions and trying to figure out how to put stuff together!) God was faithful to answer that prayer. Sometimes the neighbor girl Mikayla would come over and help me with them, just playing with them or helping me out. Sometimes she would go places with us – being that second set of hands that was so helpful, in more ways than you can imagine. Sometimes my niece's husband would come over and hang out with them or shoot hoops with them. So helpful. A girlfriend of mine had three boys, so many many times we would plan play dates together, which was fun for them, and so extremely helpful to me.

Carol Wilging

9

The year after Dallas died, I received a phone call from my niece Heather, telling me that her father, Duane, had had a heart attack in a tree stand while hunting, and did not make it. Again, another death, another shock. Duane was Dallas' closest brother, his best friend. The Jones family experiences yet another death in our family.

About a year and a half after Dallas died, I received a phone call that my sister Linda was in the hospital. She hadn't been feeling well, so she was taken to the emergency room. Within a short time, she was unconscious. Linda had endured a lot in her lifetime, a few of which were being diagnosed with Type 1 diabetes in her teens, breast cancer, and foot surgeries. My other sisters and I, as well as her son & daughter-in-law, cousins and nieces and nephews, all stood vigil at the hospital waiting for a miracle….and answers. In time we were told that she had Leukemia, a diagnosis that shocked us all. After a long day of waiting, praying, and hoping, she passed away. The very same day she entered the emergency room. Another loss. Added to the loss of my parents, my husband, my brother-in-law, now my sister, with whom I had a very close relationship. We were all in shock. And again, grief continued. Linda's oldest son, Brian, and his wife lived in New York, and they made plans to immediately get on a plane to come to Ohio. Unfortunately, by the time they arrived, Linda was already gone.

Going on with life, with my 'new normal', was not easy, but I knew God was giving me the strength to go on. I was grateful that my relationships with my stepchildren Josh and Jessica were still intact. I feared losing my relationships with them and my grandsons. I told Jessica one day that I feared losing her and the boys; that I had become Grandma because of her dad. But she immediately said, "no you didn't, you did that all on your own", meaning that she knew I had worked at my relationship with Cameron and Tony, and it existed not only because of Dallas.

Dallas was a very well-loved and well-respected man in Wadsworth. The line at his calling hours for people to pay their respects was out the door of the funeral home and down the street – for hours! I felt so loved and so special being Dallas's wife. He had chosen me!! I was Mrs. Dallas Jones! And then, after he died, my "identity" became Dallas's widow. I carried that identity with me for several years. I wore it like a badge of honor. No-one loved Dallas like I did. And no-one loved me like Dallas. I didn't know who I was anymore without him. Alone. Single. Different. My identity, which I know now is "who I am in Christ" became the survivor. The widow. Dallas's widow.

10

Time marched forward, whether I wanted it to or not. Seven years went by after Dallas died. I had a couple dates here and there, but nothing of real significance. Until I met David. A family member knew him, and asked me if he could give David my phone number. I said yes. Our first date was at a small coffee shop in Wadsworth. We fell in love very quickly, and were married within two months of meeting.

I really had prayed about this decision. It felt right. I thought, maybe incorrectly in retrospect, that God was giving me a second chance at a forever love; that this time I would be able to grow old with someone. We married at City Hall, with no-one in attendance, no family, no friends. There were a few family members I didn't even tell that I was getting married.

It wasn't long into this marriage, that I began to detect a lot of jealousy, insecurity, and anger. We lived in my condo for a while after getting married. He would wake up in the middle of the night and pick a fight with me. One night while he was angry about something, he screamed at me and began to get dressed, saying he was going to go stay at his other house. I pleaded with him to look at what he was doing! That this just was not right; we were married, and he needed to stay here and not run away. Finally, something broke through, and he decided not to leave. That was one of many, many fights we would have in the middle of the night.

Within a couple months of getting married, he started showing signs of extreme jealousy, even of the male pastoral staff I was working with at my church. Then he began to tell me how jealous he was of Dallas, who was dead, and really of no threat to him. His extreme jealousy and insecurities put a wedge in our relationship that, try as I might, could not be overcome. He would not let me ever talk about Dallas, or any of the events of the 13 years I was married to Dallas. David had been divorced, with four grown children, and of course, he was allowed to talk about them and his past. But if I dared say anything about my past, he would get very angry and give me the silent treatment for hours…or days. He said, maybe not in these exact words, that he would've rather I had been vehemently divorced than to have had a happy life with Dallas; that he wished HE could've been my one true love. He would say that he didn't want to go places together if I had been there with Dallas. One time we went to Amish Country. He questioned me as to if I'd ever gone there with Dallas. I couldn't tell him that Dallas and I had our week-long honeymoon in Amish Country or that Millersburg had been one of our favorite places. But I finally admitted that Dallas and I had been to Millersburg, and he got so angry and said "if I had known you went to Millersburg with him, I never would've gone with you." I never made him feel that I loved him any less. I was constantly reassuring him how much I loved him. That it really was possible to love two people in a lifetime. I tried to convince him that God had brought us together, that it was our time, our chance at love and lasting happiness.

No matter what I did, things never got better. We were on a steady downward spiral toward disaster, it only kept getting worse, try as I did to be a great wife and love him with everything I had. I sacrificed a lot after marrying him. We moved out of my condo. He had built a loft apartment above his business, so that is where we moved to. I gave my dog (whom I loved) to my sister Vicki. I quit my job (he wanted me to, I think just because he was so very jealous of any other relationships I had besides him). I stopped attending my church, where I had been going for years with Dallas, because I felt it would be good for our marriage if we found our own church, a place where no-one knew us, no memories of Dallas. And in addition to all those sacrifices, he really didn't want me staying connected to Dallas's family. Even though they were MY family for 20 years!! He literally said, "hanging on to them was hanging on to *him*." I couldn't make him see the illogicalness of that – they were MY family. But to try and honor him and my marriage, I began to pull away from them. Finding excuses to decline invitations. One time we went to a Christmas party at one of Dallas's brothers, and I thought it had been a lovely evening, that everything had gone fine and he had a great time. BUT when we got home, all his jealousies and insecurities came flooding out. Which only made me pull away from the Jones family even more.

I had a great number of friends and family that I confided my marital troubles to. Thank God for those people who knew what was really going on inside my marriage and home. Some evenings I would text them and say "we are fighting, please pray, don't text back." I couldn't risk him looking at my phone and learning that I was sharing our troubles with other people. It was only The Lord that got me through my marriage. I begged David to go see a marriage counselor with me. He adamantly refused each time I asked. I knew that he was so prideful that he couldn't admit to anyone, let alone a counselor, that he had issues that he needed to deal with. I would pray and pray that things would get better, and sometimes they did. But he never truly exhibited any lasting change. He would always want to fight, feel sorry for himself, and give me the silent treatment when he wasn't yelling at me. I went back to drinking alcohol while he and I were on our honeymoon in California. I had stopped drinking for a couple years before I met David, but alcohol had become my friend again – anything to help me endure this horrible marriage I had found myself in. I wished I could rewind time and make different decisions (as in not marry him.) I would pray and pray and pray – and beg God to "make me a widow again". The thought of his death brought me comfort and hope. I know that sounds terrible, but when you're in that much emotional pain, death looks like the easiest solution.

Josh and Maria, my stepson and his wife, and my sisters, Patty and Vicki, knew everything. They liked David in the beginning. They were supportive of our relationship and encouraged me to take a risk and give myself wholeheartedly to a new life with him. But I shared the truth with them while I was going through it, and it infuriated Josh to see his stepmom being treated like this. Finally after months and months of trying to make my marriage work, of trying to convince him that I had chosen him, that I loved him, that God had brought us together, I just couldn't do it any longer. I felt like an abused woman, even though there were no physical blows or bruises. It was emotional, mental, and verbal abuse. I was beaten down. Weary. Regretful. Disappointed. Fearful. I never knew what would set him off. He would go for hours and hours giving me the silent treatment. We would fight. I would always try to get us back on the same page. I would implore him to see "we are on the same team!!!"

Josh encouraged me to leave him. I tried once, and David convinced me to give it another month. I agreed. But I told him

I was going to go see a counselor, by myself. He had no problem with that. He probably thought the counselor would convince me that I was wrong, that as a Christian, I should stay and endure it. After all, in David's mind, if he wasn't beating me or cheating on me, I had no grounds to leave.

My counselor, Ruth, who is a Christian, helped me see things clearly. Things got worse after I started seeing a counselor. And one last time, a little over a year after marrying David, I asked him again if he would go with me to Christian marriage counseling. Again, his answer was no. So I said "if you're not willing to see a marriage counselor with me, then I think we should separate." His response was the same as it always had been before: "Okay, then we'll separate."

I found an apartment. And in the course of three days, I got all my belongings out of his apartment, and left. He begged me to come back. It was the hardest decision of my life. But I knew in my gut that he was never going to change, that he was never going to admit his problems and insecurities and issues.

Josh and Maria, as well as my sisters and friends that had walked this journey with me, who knew the TRUTH about the horrible pain I was in and all that I had been going through in this marriage were very supportive and happy for me.

Carol Wilging

11

Three months after David and I separated, we had our divorce hearing and I found myself alone yet again. The last few months of my marriage to David I had been sick a lot, bronchitis and laryngitis to name a couple things. The laryngitis just would not clear up, I saw my doctor a couple times about it, and nothing she suggested seemed to help. I saw a specialist about it, and he said I had a paralyzed vocal cord. We made plans to do some type of surgical procedure that was to fix the paralysis of this vocal cord. The date of the surgery was set.

The day after my divorce hearing, on August 10, 2017, I was flying to Dallas, Texas with Cameron to visit Ron & Yoka, one of Dallas's brothers and his wife. Yoka and I talked often about my problems with David. The day of our flight I noticed that I was suddenly talking clear as a bell, the laryngitis was completely gone! I knew in my gut, in my spirit, that God had healed me! I had lost my voice while I was with David, physically and figuratively, but as soon as the legal tie was severed with him, healing came. I truly did see it as a spiritual sign that God had set me free and rescued me, and healed me. Every time I see the word "rescue" in the bible, and it is there a lot, I circle it. Because I truly believe that God DID rescue me. I felt like an Israelite who was in bondage in Egypt, and after crying out to the Lord over and over, He finally set me free. God loved me so much He didn't want to see me endure this pain for the rest of my life and He rescued me.

Carol Wilging

12

The loss of a marriage….not due to death this time, due to divorce. I returned to my church, and felt judged. Was it my imagination? Was it a misperception that somehow I was viewed differently? When you lose your husband due to death, you receive sympathy and encouraging words. Maybe even food brought to your door or invited over for a meal. But few are the encouraging words and sympathy when you get a divorce. It doesn't usually warrant a meal. I knew the scripture that says "God hates divorce." Every believer who finds themselves in a horrible marriage knows that verse. But I knew the Holy Spirit, and I knew that He saw my pain and what I was going through, and He cared. I believe He allowed me to leave and get a divorce. He wasn't condemning me for it. Divorce is not the unpardonable sin that separates us from God's grace. He hates divorce because He is the author of marriage, so of course He would hate it. He knows that divorce will hurt. And He hates it because He knows the pain it causes His children, not just the partners of the marriage, but the ripple effects it can have on all those around us. Sometimes children are involved. And the emotional pain is far-reaching, and long-lasting. Our heartache and emotional pain break His heart for us. But He is The Healer.

Inside I was grieving and sorrowful, almost as much as when Dallas died. Almost. The pain was often times unbearable. Again, as when Dallas died, I found myself sitting on my office floor in my new apartment with my bible on my lap, crying and crying, pouring my heart out to God. And once again I received the comfort from The God of All Comfort.

There is a song by Mercy Me called "The Hurt and the Healer". It says *"so here I am, what's left of me, where Glory meets my suffering. I'm alive. Even though a part of me has died. You take my heart and breathe it back to life. I fall into Your arms open wide, when the hurt and The Healer collide. Breathe, sometimes I feel it's all that I can do. Pain so deep that I can hardly move. Just keep my eyes completely fixed on You. Lord take hold and pull me through..."* I would play this song over and over, because I just love the words – where *MY* hurt and *THE HEALER* collide – when His comfort and presence and grace are able to so completely overpower the hurt and pain that you find yourself in and supernaturally and miraculously the pain lessens and the hurt begins to heal.

I had fallen madly in love with David. I thought we would grow old together. There is a song by Little Big Town called Better Man. It says, *"I wish I could forget when it was magic. The bravest thing I ever did was run. Sometimes in the middle of the night I can feel you again, but I just miss you and I just wish you were a better man. I know why I had to say goodbye like the back of my hand, and I just miss you and I just wish you were a better man. And it's always on your terms, I'm hanging on every careless word, hoping it might turn sweet again, like it was in the beginning."* Even though I knew I had done the right thing in leaving, that the choice to leave had God's blessing and favor, I still missed him. I couldn't stop replaying all the good times and all the memories. In times of doubt, I began to write on colored index cards every single instance where I had been abused, silenced, fought with, controlled, and made to feel bad when I said the wrong thing. The cards just kept growing. And I would re-read them, to remind myself what my reality had actually been, not some romanticized version of our love story. It's a difficult journey to grieve someone who is still alive, someone who you secretly still love. It's paradoxical; loving someone who acted like they hated you, being set free but often looking back on the bondage.

God gave me the strength to go on. Surrounded by family and friends who knew the truth, who supported me, and who were extremely thankful for my freedom helped me have the courage to even want to go on. I let myself stay unemployed for eight months, giving myself time to heal, grieve, and ponder where God might be leading me now. What was His will for me? What was I supposed to do? Life after divorce is difficult when you live in a "couples world". Most of my friends were married. Most of the places I might get invited to I had to go to alone, like weddings, funerals, family gatherings. It became necessary to fight against jealousy and envy, when all around me were people who still had their husbands, children, grandchildren, houses. You're tempted to ask God WHY? Why was His plan that my life and journey would look so differently than everyone else's? There's never an answer to the why question, other than "trust". I'm not meant to know, I'm only meant to follow God, learn His ways, and trust that He knows what He's doing. And maybe the answer lies that in trials and heartache and grief is found a more intimate connection with Jesus and His Spirit than if I had never gone through the trial and the pain. If your faith is not tested, how does it get proved genuine? If you don't need comfort, how do you get to know The Comforter? I grew to learn that joy and peace were only to be found in Him.

At the end of 2017 God led me to get a job at an independent living senior care facility in my town. I loved this job so much, and it was exactly what I needed. After a few years, God led me out of that job, and led me to a receptionist job at a hair salon very close to my home. It was a perfect fit! I got to be around people, both clients and coworkers, where I could give words of encouragement and a listening ear. Many of our clients were elderly, so this job sort of flowed over from my previous one at the senior care facility. It brought me new friends, and a new sense of purpose.

13

My relationships with Josh and Jessica and their families continued to be strong after my divorce from David. I worked hard to maintain my connection with them, and specifically at that time, with Cameron and Tony, my grandsons. I wanted to have a strong, growing relationship with them so much. I initiated and pursued.

I felt God leading me to once again give up alcohol, because He didn't want me making it an idol and turning to it for emotional support. He wanted to be the *only* One that I ran to, and not use alcohol to try and numb the pain I found myself in. So in February 2020 I made the decision to stop drinking. There is a special verse in Jeremiah 17:5-8 that talks about how if you depend on flesh, either your own or someone else, you will be cursed. But that if you turn to the Lord and rely on Him alone, you will be blessed. Those verses spoke to me after Dallas died and also post-divorce. I couldn't turn to people to try and give me what I needed; I could only rely on the Lord with my whole heart.

Cameron and I got closer and closer. As Cameron became a teenager, life at home got stressful for him. His mom appreciated my role in his life, and allowed me to help out, like paying for haircuts or driving him places. I found myself severely codependent with him, wanting to rescue him from all of life's trials, and unable to say no to him. The next few years he got into some trouble, as a lot of teenagers do. Without "Grandpa" to kneel in prayer with, I prayed fervently for him, and little by little, he got through it. Not without some serious consequences.

As my relationship with Cameron stayed strong, my relationship with his mom diminished. I think the help she so graciously appreciated for years began to be resented. I don't know if it was jealousy, or anger, or her just needing to set some boundaries, but Jessica withdrew from me, and didn't feel the need to stay in a relationship with me. It hurt deeply. Many prayers and tears cried about it. I always felt that Dallas would've wanted me to stay in relationship with his kids, and I did that to the best of my ability. But I finally had to realize that there were many, many people who loved me and wanted to be in relationship with me, so I could not take it personally that she chose not to pursue me or stay close to me. We all have a path to follow, we all have a different journey. It didn't make me "less than" that she didn't need me or want to be in relationship with me. I knew I had a clear conscience before God, that I had been myself with her and had loved her with all humility and sincerity. I used to mentally itemize all I had done for her for 25 years, feeling so hurt that after all I'd done for her and her children how could she not want me in her life? I pray for her often, but I have learned how to "let go", and go on with my life.

14

Early 2020 brings about the Coronavirus pandemic. Covid. Life as we all knew it ceased to exist. Suddenly we were being told to distance ourselves from others. Stay home. It was unlike anything we had ever encountered. It perpetuates separateness and loneliness and isolation. And it promoted division – are you anti-vaccine or pro-vaccine. Anti-mask or pro-mask. Social distancing or partying it up. It took years, literally years, for us to all adjust and get through it. Life was never again to really be the same. Restaurants and small businesses forced to close. All of a sudden, places of business couldn't find workers. Were people enjoying the free money the government was giving us, and now we didn't need to work? Even after the free money ended, it seemed that everywhere you turned you would see "NOW HIRING" signs.

During Covid, Josh and Maria and their daughter Ava lived right across the street from me. I would long for days of good weather so that we could all be outside and have social interaction! On Christmas Day of 2020, we were celebrating in my garage! As restrictions lifted after several months, it brought so much joy to be able to have them in my house again, or me in theirs. It felt like a prison sentence to not be able to socialize inside houses. Of course, not everyone felt led to comply with these government-imposed restrictions, but for those of us that did, it literally stunk!

In March/April of 2020, right as Covid is ramping up, I began to have some physical symptoms that kept getting worse. As I'm telling my daughter-in-law Maria about them, she informs me that every single symptom was that of diabetes! She urgently tells me to go to the drugstore and get a glucometer to check my sugar. My first reading was 444! I already had a doctors appointment on the books, but because of Covid and social distancing, it was via Telehealth, on my computer. My doctor is concerned about my symptoms and glucose numbers, so I'm called in for an in-person appointment, where of course I have to wear a mask due to Covid. I was diagnosed with Type 1 Diabetes, at the age of 58! I'm now forced to take insulin shots and see an endocrinologist. Never in a million years did I think I would have to deal with this. My sister Linda had been a diabetic, and to think that once again my life will never be the same was sort of frightening and daunting. Now I had to stop and think about every single thing I would put in my mouth. How much insulin to take. How to manage this new illness and keep myself alive? It would've been even more overwhelming than it already was had it not been for the fact that Maria is Type 1 Diabetic, and she would become my "coach", and answer all the questions I had, which were many.

The Fall of 2020 brings another whammy – I am diagnosed with a rare form of breast cancer called Adenoid Cystic Carcinoma. One of its symptoms besides being slow growing is that it causes pain, which I had for years. So in November of 2020 I undergo a lumpectomy, but due to the fact that they were unsuccessful in getting clear margins, I had to have it repeated two more times. Following that I had a few months of radiation. Once again, God was faithful, and I am cancer free!

15

In 2022 Jessica made plans to move out of her home when Cameron was 19, so he came to live with me for just under a year. I was thankful to God for allowing me to be here for him, and help him in very practical ways to continue to learn how to enter adulthood. He wasn't ready to be out on his own, and he was grateful that he had a safe place to land, with his grandma that he knew had always been there for him and always would. About seven months after he moved in, I felt it was time for him to be out on his own, so I encouraged him to do so, and he found his first apartment. So many things to learn at that age, things about banks, checking accounts, credit cards, paying bills on time, filing a tax return, just to name a few. Cameron's dad, Matt, had always been a steady, godly influence in his life and I was grateful for that. But Matt had gotten remarried and had a new family, so Cameron didn't really want to go live with him when Jessica moved. I hadn't asked for this parental role, it was sort of thrust upon me, but I welcomed him with open arms. My continual prayer: Help me to be Grandma without Grandpa.

It's now 2024. My grandsons are now 18 and 21 as I write this. And I have the blessing of getting to be "Grams" to Josh and Maria's two children, their daughter Ava and son Noah. Psalm 68:5-6 says that "God is a father to the fatherless and a defender of widows. And that God sets the lonely in families." How grateful to God I have been for the last 29 years for the families God has placed me in. In addition to my own parents and sisters, I had the joy of being in Dallas's big family, a church family, workplace families, Jessica's family, and then ultimately in family with Josh and Maria and their children. Never having had my own children, I have always been very grateful to God for giving me the gift of grandparenting.

As this story comes to a close, I am grateful to God for the journey I've been on, the path The Lord has charted for the past 63 years. I am thankful for God's faithfulness through it all. The joys and the sorrows. The mountains and the valleys. The hard places and those of ease. His grace and His presence and His Word have been my anchor. His love and joy have filled my heart and given me hope. And I am thankful for the many, many scripture verses that I have clung to and that sustained me all along the way.

To God be the Glory. All praise to Him!!

THE END

If you have any questions or need any additional information, contact
Advantage Books at info@advbooks.com

For additional copies of this book or for the eBook version visit

advbookstore.com
or
amazon.com

we bring dreams to life ™

www.ingramcontent.com/pod-product-compliance
Lightning Source LLC
Chambersburg PA
CBHW070749050426
42449CB00010B/2394